WELCOME TO THE COMPLETE CRICKET QUIZ BOOK

Lunar Press is a privately-run publishing company which cares greatly about the accuracy of its content.

As many questions in this quiz book are subject to change, please email us at lunarpresspublishers@gmail.com if you notice any inaccuracies to help us keep our questions as up-to-date as possible.

Happy Quizzing!

CONTENTS

ANSWERS

TERMINOLOGY

1. A player that can both bat and bowl is known as what?

2. Batting average is worked out by dividing the total number of runs scored by a batsman by what?

3. What is a bye?

4. If a batter 'carries their bat' what have they done?
a. Scored a double century
b. An opening batsman is not dismissed when the team innings closes
c. Batted for one-hour
d. Scored more than half the team's runs

5. What is the name of the player who stands behind the wicket while a team is fielding?

6. What is the term used when a captain voluntarily brings their sides innings to a close?

7. If a batter is out for a duck, how many runs have they scored?
a. 0   b. 1   c. Less than 10   d. 100

8. A delivery by a finger spin bowler that spins in the opposite direction to the stock ball is known as what?
a. Doosra   b. Googly   c. Slider

9. What is the method used to determine the winner of a limited overs game affected by weather?

10. The average number of runs given away by a bowler per over is known as their what?

11. What is a maiden over?

12. The term NRR stands for what?

13. What is the term used when a batter fails to make contact with the wicket with their bat beyond the popping crease, and turns back for an additional run?
a. No run   b. One run   c. One short   d. No stride

14. What are the white boards placed behind a bowler off the pitch known as?

15. What position are you fielding if you are standing on the off-side next to the wicketkeeper?
a. Slip   b. Gully   c. Mid on   d. Fine leg

16. What is the name of the longest form of cricket?

17. What is it called when the batter is out because they do not occupy the crease within 3 minutes of the fall of the last wicket?

18. DRS is an acronym for which technology used in international cricket?

19. What is the name of the officials who adjudicate play?

20. If a wicket is referred to as a 'road' this suggests what?

21. How many stumps form a wicket?
a. 2   b. 3   c. 4   d. 5

22. What is the name for a short-pitched delivery, which is generally pitched by a fast bowler, which bounces once and comes at the batter at head height?

23. Which player on each team is often referred to as a skipper?

24. The area between deep mid-wicket and wide long-on is referred to as what?
a. Horse corner   b. Pig corner   c. Tiger corner   d. Cow corner

25. What does the ball do when it reverse swings?

STADIUMS

1. Which stadium is known as the Home of Cricket?

2. How many people can the largest cricket ground in the world, Narendra Modi Stadium in Ahmedabad, India, hold?
a. 109,000   b. 117,000   c. 126,000   d. 132,000

3. Of the top 10 largest cricket stadiums in the world, how many are in India?
a. 3   b. 5   c. 7   d. 9

4. The Gabba is an Australian cricket ground located in which city?
a. Brisbane   b. Melbourne   c. Sydney   d. Perth

5. In which year did the National Bank Cricket Arena in Karachi, Pakistan, host its first Test match?
a. 1952   b. 1956   c. 1960   d. 1964

6. What is the name of New Zealand's largest cricket stadium that holds 50,000 people?
a. Sky Stadium   b. Forsyth Barr Stadium
c. Mt Smart Stadium   d. Eden Park

7. In which Caribbean country is the Kensington Oval located?
a. Barbados   b. Jamaica   c. Antigua   d. Guyana

8. Which English cricket ground shares the same name as the football ground in the same city?

9. Which country has the largest cricket stadium in Africa?
a. Kenya   b. South Africa   c. Zimbabwe   d. Tunisia

10. Mahinda Rajapaksa International Cricket Stadium is the biggest cricket stadium in its country, being able to hold 35,010 people, but in which country would you find it?
a. Nepal   b. Sri Lanka   c. Pakistan   d. Bangladesh

11. Which stadium in Wales hosted the country's first Ashes Test in 2009?

12. Where do the Mumbai Indians IPL team play their home games?

13. Which ground in Kingston, Jamaica do West Indies play their home games?
a. Sabina Park   b. Warner Park   c. Mindoo Park   d. Windsor Park

14. What is the name of the Sydney-based cricket ground converted to a football stadium in 2015?

15. What caused the Queen Elizabeth II Park in Christchurch, New Zealand, to be destroyed in 2011?

16. In which British city would you find County Cricket Ground, with a capacity of 21,000 people?
a. Manchester   b. London   c. York   d. Birmingham

17. Which non Test playing nation has a larger ground than England?

18. In which English city is the Rose Bowl located?
a. Liverpool   b. Bristol   c. Southampton   d. Oxford

19. Which is the largest cricket ground in Perth?

20. Which of the Sydney based BBL sides play at Sydney Showgrounds?

GUESS THE PLAYER

1. This player was born in Pietermaritzburg, South Africa in 1980, but went on to play 104 times for England in Tests, scoring 8181 runs.
a. Andrew Strauss   b. Kevin Pietersen   c. Jonathan Trott

2. Between 1999-2008 this wicket-keeper batter scored 5570 runs in Test matches with a highest score of 204*.
a. Brad Haddin   b. Ian Healy   c. Adam Gilchrist

3. This Sri Lankan Test batter, who made his debut in 1997, racked up 11,814 at an average of 49.84.
a. Kumar Sangakkara   b. Mahela Jayawardene   c. Sanath Jayasuriya

4. This bowler took 519 Test wickets for West Indies in his 18-year Test career having bowled over 30,000 balls, as well as captaining the West Indies in 22 Test matches.
a. Courtney Walsh   b. Curtly Ambrose   c. Malcolm Marshall

5. This England Test bowler took 226 wickets at an economy rate of 3.22 between 2002 -2009.
a. Andrew Flintoff   b. Matthew Hoggard   c. Steve Harmison

6. Which English Test batter scored 8231 in a career spanning 15 years, but only scored ten 6s in that time?
a. David Gower   b. Michael Atherton   c. Graham Thorpe

7. Which batter has scored the most Test runs in history?

8. Who is the highest scoring Australian batter in Test matches?
a. Steve Waugh   b. Allan Border   c. Steve Smith   d. Ricky Ponting

9. Sri Lanka's Muttiah Muralitharan is the highest Test wicket taker of all time, but which bowler is third on the overall wicket taking list, and the highest of all fast bowlers?

10. This New Zealand all-rounder was born in 1979, played 113 Tests, took 362 runs, as well as scoring 4531 runs in his career.
a. Ken Rutherford   b. Daniel Vettori
c. Nathan Astle   d. Chris Martin

11. This Australian bowler played between 1996-2006. He took 259 wickets and scored an unbeaten 201 in his final Test match against Bangladesh in 2006.
a. Jason Gillespie   b. Stuart MacGill   c. Brett Lee   d. Simon Katich

12. Who is Australia's highest wicket-taker in Tests, with 708 wickets?

13. What is the name of the West Indies Test all-rounder who scored 8032 runs and took 235 wickets between 1954-1974?

14. Which former South African Test bowler retired in 2019 with 439 wickets from just 93 Test matches?

15. Which England Test player took 307 wickets between 1952-1965?
a. Peter May   b. Trevor Bailey   c. Fred Trueman   d. Alec Bedser

16. Which Australian pace bowler finished their Test career having played 124 Tests, taking 563 wickets?
a. Brett Lee   b. Mitchell Johnson   c. Glenn McGrath

17. Which former Pakistani Test player took 414 wickets bowling left arm pace?

18. Which English Test all-rounder was known as Beefy?

19. Which player took 373 wickets at 23.56 in Tests for Pakistan between 1989-2003?
a. Ijaz Ahmed   b. Moin Khan   c. Inzamam-ul-Haq   d. Waqar Younis

20. Which Australian Test bowler, born in 1949, took 355 wickets in just 70 Tests?

21. Which Australian T20 batter, who played 103 matches, has a highest score of 172 in internationals?
a. Glenn Maxwell   b. Aaron Finch   c. Steve Smith   d. David Warner

22. Which former Pakistani batter has exactly 10,099 runs in Tests, giving him the best record of all Pakistani cricketers in Test cricket?
a. Inzamam-ul-Haq   b. Mohammad Yousuf
c. Younis Khan   d. Javed Miandad

23. Which English Test cricketer, born in 1987, made his debut in 2014 and played for England's Test team until 2021, amassing 2,914 runs in this time?

24. This player is a Guyanese-British cricketer who is thought to be one of the greatest captains of all time. He made his Test debut in 1966 and went on to score 7,515 runs in Tests.
a. Deryck Murray   b. Gordon Greenidge
c. Viv Richards   d. Clive Lloyd

25. This player made his Test debut on the 2nd of April 1988 v Pakistan, and played his last Test on the 31st of August 2000 v England. During this time he took 405 wickets, and scored 1,439 runs.

GUESS THE MATCH

You will be given the statistics of one player from the Test match. You must then work out the opponents and the year in which the game was played.

1. Rehan Ahmed took 2/89 & 5/48 for England against which team?
a. Pakistan, 2022   b. Sri Lanka, 2019
c. Zimbabwe, 2018   d. Bangladesh, 2021

2. Chris Gayle scored 333 runs in West Indies' only innings against which team?
a. India, 2004   b. England, 2014
c. Bangladesh, 2012   d. Sri Lanka, 2010

3. Devon Malcolm took 1/81 & 9/57 for England against which team?
a. New Zealand, 1982   b. India, 1997
c. South Africa, 1994   d. West Indies, 1989

4. Hamish Amla scored 311 runs in South Africa's only innings against which team?
a. England, 2012   b. India, 2015
c. New Zealand, 2007   d. Pakistan, 2009

5. Stuart Broad took 8/15 & 1/36 for England against which team?
a. Zimbabwe, 2011   b. Sri Lanka, 2016
c. Ireland, 2019   d. Australia, 2015

6. Virender Sehwag scored 309 runs in India's only innings against which team?
a. West Indies, 1995   b. Sri Lanka, 2008
c. England, 2010   d. Pakistan, 2004

7. Rangana Herath took 9/127 & 5/57 for Sri Lanka against which team?
a. England, 2009   b. Pakistan, 2014
c. New Zealand, 2011   d. South Africa, 2007

8. Brendon McCullum scored 8 & 302 runs for New Zealand against which team?
a. Australia, 2007   b. South Africa, 2016
c. England, 2012   d. India, 2014

9. Imran Khan took 8/58 & 6/58 for Pakistan against which team?
a. West Indies, 1988   b. Sri Lanka, 1982
c. India, 1978   d. Australia, 1980

10. VVS Laxman scored 59 & 281 for India against which team?
a. South Africa, 2000   b. England, 1997
c. Australia, 2001   d. Pakistan, 2004

11. Devendra Bishoo took 2/125 & 8/49 for West Indies against which team?
a. Ireland, 2018   b. Zimbabwe, 2013
c. India, 2009   d. Pakistan, 2016

12. Graeme Smith scored 277 & 85 for South Africa against which team?
a. England, 2003   b. England, 1998   c. Pakistan, 2007   d. India, 2005

13. Mitchell Johnson took 8/61 & 3/98 for Australia against which team?
a. Bangladesh, 2004   b. New Zealand, 2009
c. Sri Lanka, 2005   d. South Africa, 2008

14. Adam Voges scored 269 runs in Australia's only innings against which team?
a. Bangladesh, 2011   b. West Indies, 2015
c. Pakistan, 2017   d. England, 2012

15. Shane Warne took 3/39 & 8/71 for Australia against which team?
a. India, 1990   b. West Indies, 1997
c. New Zealand, 1999   d. England, 1994

16. Marlon Samuels scored 260 in 455 balls for West Indies against which team?
a. India, 2008   b. India, 2014
c. Bangladesh, 2012   d. South Africa, 2010

17. Merv Hughes took 5/130 & 8/87 for Australia against which team?
a. West Indies, 1988   b. England, 1981
c. New Zealand, 1985   d. Pakistan, 1990

18. Wasim Akram scored 257 runs in Pakistan's only innings against which team?
a. Sri Lanka, 2000   b. West Indies, 1994
c. South Africa, 1992   d. Zimbabwe, 1998

19. Paul Strang took 8/109 & 2/49 for Zimbabwe against which team?
a. Australia, 2000   b. New Zealand, 2000
c. England, 2000   d. Bangladesh, 2000

20. Joe Root scored 254 & 71 for England against which team?
a. Zimbabwe, 2013   b. West Indies, 2017
c. Australia, 2014   d. Pakistan, 2016

21. Saqlain Mushtaq took 8/164 & 1/14 for Pakistan against which team?
a. India, 1994   b. Sri Lanka, 1990
c. England, 2000   d. South Africa, 1995

22. Ben Stokes scored 258 & 26 for England against which team?
a. Zimbabwe, 2014   b. South Africa, 2016
c. New Zealand, 2018   d. India, 2015

23. Michael Holding took 8/92 & 6/57 for West Indies against which team?
a. England, 1976   b. Australia, 1969
c. South Africa, 1965   d. India, 1979

24. Wally Hammond scored 251 & did not bat for England against which team?

a. Australia, 1919   b. South Africa, 1931

c. Australia, 1928   d. New Zealand, 1933

25. Matthew Hayden scored 380 in Australia's only innings against which team?

a. Bangladesh, 2000   b. Zimbabwe, 2003

c. Pakistan, 1995   d. West Indies, 1993

THE ASHES

1. How many centuries did Alastair Cook score in Ashes Tests?
a. 4   b. 5   c. 6   d. 7

2. In which year did Steve Smith score his first Ashes century?
a. 2011   b. 2012   c. 2013   d. 2014

3. Which wicket-keeper scored his only Ashes century at the SCG in 2011?

4. Who is the highest run scorer in Ashes history?
a. Jack Hobbs   b. Steve Waugh   c. Allan Border   d. Don Bradman

5. Which commentator said the following when commentating on a shot by Ian Botham in the Ashes? "Don't bother looking for that, let alone chasing it. That's gone straight into the confectionary stall and out again."

6. Where is the Ashes urn kept?

7. Which Australian bowler took 31 wickets in the 1993 Ashes tour?
a. Merv Hughes   b. Craig McDermott   c. Greg Matthews

8. Which player tackled a pitch invader at the WACA in 1982?
a. Geoff Lawson   b. Rodney Hogg
c. Dean Jones   d. Terry Alderman

9. How many runs did Wally Hammond score in the 1928-29 Ashes series?
a. 677   b. 756   c. 841   d. 905

10. What is the Ashes urn made of?

11. In which year did the Ashes officially begin?
a. 1872   b. 1882   c. 1892   d. 1902

12. Where was the first Ashes Test played?
a. The Oval, London   b. Old Trafford, Manchester
c. MCG, Melbourne   d. Adelaide Oval, Adelaide

13. Which side won the first 8 Ashes series?

14. Won was the captain of England in the first-ever Ashes Test?
a. Hugh Massie   b. Albert Hornby   c. Fred Spofforth   d. Ivo Bligh

15. How many series did Australia win in a row before England triumphed in 2005?
a. 6   b. 7   c. 8   d. 9

16. How many matches did England win in the 2010-11 Ashes series in Australia?
a. 1   b. 2   c. 3   d. 4

17. Which captain has the most Ashes wins?
a. Mike Brearley   b. Allan Border
c. Don Bradman   d. Ricky Ponting

18. As of January 2023, in which year did Australia last win the Ashes 5-0?
a. 2021-22   b. 2017-18   c. 2013-14   d. 2006-07

19. How many runs did England win by in the 2005 Edgbaston Ashes Test?
a. 1   b. 2   c. 4   d. 244

20. Which England batsman was dismissed by Shane Warne's 'Ball of the Century' in the 1993 Ashes series?
a. Mike Gatting   b. Graham Gooch
c. Graham Thorpe   d. John Emburey

21. Which English spinner took 19 of the 20 wickets in the 1956 Ashes Test in Manchester?

22. What was the name of the substitute fielder who ran Ricky Ponting out in the 2005 Trent Bridge Ashes Test?
a. Paul Collingwood   b. Gary Pratt   c. Mark Hoggard

23. Which Australian spinner scored 98 runs batting at number 11 in the 2013 Trent Bridge Ashes Test?
a. Ashton Agar   b. Nathan Lyon   c. Xavier Doherty

24. In his final Test, which English leg spinner dismissed Don Bradman for a duck (Zero)?
a. Ken Farnes   b. Hedley Verity   c. Freddie Brown   d. Eric Hollies

25. What was different about the 4th Test in Sydney during the 1882/83 Ashes series?
a. They used a pink ball   b. They played on separate pitches
c. They had light up bails   d. It was interrupted by a mob of emus

26. Which English player tried to speed up the end of Australia's innings by kicking the ball over the boundary to expose a tailender to the bowling?
a. Sir Len Hutton   b. Geoffrey Boycott   c. David Gower

27. How many Tests were played in the 1970/71 Ashes series in Australia?
a. 3   b. 4   c. 6   d. 7

28. How many runs did Sir Donald Bradman average in Ashes Tests?
a. 84.63   b. 89.78   c. 94.33   d. 99.09

29. What was the final series score in the 2005 Ashes?
a. 2-1 England   b. 4-0 Australia   c. 3-0 England   d. 3-1 Australia

30. What is the Ashes urn said to contain?

31. Which Australian bowler is the leading Ashes wicket-taker?
a. Dennis Lillee   b. Glenn McGrath   c. Shane Warne

32. Who has taken the most 5 wicket hauls in Ashes Tests?
a. James Anderson   b. Ian Botham   c. Sydney Barnes

33. Which player has captained the most Ashes Tests?
a. Alastair Cook   b. Allan Border
c. Ricky Ponting   d. Michael Vaughan

34. Jack Leach's 1 not out, in the 2019 Headingly Test that England won, came off how many deliveries?
a. 21   b. 27   c. 33   d. 39

35. Who was the England captain that won the toss at the Gabba in 2002, but mistakenly chose to bowl first?

36. Which of the following is Australia's largest margin of victory in an Ashes Test?
a. An innings and 111   b. An innings and 241   c. An innings and 322

37. How many wickets did Mitchell Johnson take in the 2013-14 Ashes series?
a. 25   b. 32   c. 37   d. 44

38. How many runs did Ben Stokes score in the 2019 Headingly Test to win the game for England?
a. 121*   b. 135*   c. 148*   d. 156*

39. Where is the famous Boxing Day Test played between Australia and England every 4 years?

40. Which of the following players has played Test matches for both Australia and England (not both Ashes)?
a. Alfred Shaw   b. Billy Midwinter   c. Dave Gregory

41. Why was Peter Chappell jailed during the 1975 Ashes series?
a. Attacking a player   b. Bribing an official   c. Sabotaging the pitch

42. Which Australian international has played Ashes Tests but zero first class matches in Australia?
a. Brett Lee   b. Sammy Woods   c. Jack Gregory

43. Which player bowled the longest spell in Ashes Tests of 51.1 overs?
a. Tom Veivers   b. Graeme Swann   c. Shane Warne

44. Which player took 5 wickets in 7 Ashes balls across the 1998 Perth Test and 2001 Edgbaston Test?

45. Alick Bannerman faced the most amount of deliveries in a single day in the Sydney Test during the 1981-82 series. How many did he face?
a. 232   b. 310   c. 389   d. 423

46. How many runs did Graeme Swann concede in his final over of Ashes cricket, that lead to him retiring midway through the series?
a. 19   b. 20   c. 21   d. 22

47. In the 2013/14 Ashes series, which player was not dismissed throughout the whole series?
a. Michael Clarke   b. Ryan Harris   c. Steve Smith   d. Nathan Lyon

48. Who is the only player to umpire an Ashes Test before playing in one?
a. Patrick McShane   b. George McShane   c. Steve McShane

49. What grade of ball was delivered and used in the first innings of the 1925 Melbourne Ashes Test?
a. Grade 1   b. Grade 2   c. Grade 3   d. Grade 4

50. In his 22 Ashes Test's, which player bowled 9,164 deliveries but no wides or no balls?
a. Bill O'Reilly   b. Clarrie Grimmett   c. Warwick Armstrong

WORLD TEST CHAMPIONSHIP

1. Which year did the World Test Championship begin?
a. 2017   b. 2018   c. 2019   d. 2020

2. In which year was the first World Test Championship final held?
a. 2018   b. 2019   c. 2020   d. 2021

3. Who won the first World Test Championship final?
a. New Zealand   b. India   c. Australia   d. Pakistan

4. Which player was Man of the Final in the first World Test Championship final?
a. Virat Kohli   b. Kyle Jamieson   c. Devon Conway   d. Shubman Gill

5. Who is the overall tournament top scorer, as of January 2023, with 3575 runs?
a. Steve Smith   b. Virat Kohli   c. Joe Root   d. Faf du Plessis

6. Where was the first ever final of the World Test Championship held?

7. Who was the overall tournament highest wicket-taker with 71?
a. Pat Cummins   b. Ravichandran Ashwin
c. Kagiso Rabada   d. Trent Boult

8. In which year was the first World Test Championship supposed to be held, where it would have replaced the ICC Champions Trophy?
a. 2007   b. 2009   c. 2011   d. 2013

9. What date did the second World Test Championship start?
a. 4th August 2021   b. 27th August 2021   c. 17th September 2021

10. Which cricketer had the best bowling averages of the first World Test Championship?
a. Ishant Sharma   b. James Anderson   c. Umesh Yadav   d. Axar Patel

T20 WORLD CUP

1. Which nation hosted the 2016 T20 World Cup?
a. Bangladesh   b. India   c. West Indies   d. Sri Lanka

2. In which country was the first T20 World Cup held?
a. England   b. South Africa   c. Australia   d. India

3. How many runs did Braithwaite score off the final over of the 2016 T20 World Cup bowled by Ben Stokes?
a. 20   b. 22   c. 24   d. 26

4. In which year was the first T20 World Cup hosted?
a. 2003   b. 2005   c. 2007   d. 2009

5. Who won the 2022 T20 World Cup?
a. England   b. South Africa   c. India   d. Sri Lanka

6. As of 2022, how many times have Pakistan played in the final of the T20 World Cup?
a. 2   b. 3   c. 4   d. 5

7. At which stadium was the final of the 2010 T20 World Cup, hosted in the West Indies, held?

8. Which batter scored 123 against Bangladesh in 2012 for New Zealand?
a. Ross Taylor   b. Kane Williamson
c. Rob Nicol   d. Brendon McCullum

9. As of 2022, which cricketer has the most sixes in T20 World Cup history?
a. Rohit Sharma   b. David Warner   c. Chris Gayle   d. Yuvraj Singh

10. England chased 168 set by India in the 2022 T20 World Cup semi-final by scoring 170-0. Which two batters scored England's runs?

11. Which Sri Lankan bowler took the most wickets in the 2021 T20 World Cup?
a. Wanindu Hasaranga   b. Maheesh Theekshana
c. Dushmantha Chameera

12. Which player was the Player of the Tournament at the 2009 T20 World Cup?
a. Kevin Pietersen   b. Brendon McCullum   c. Tillakaratne Dilshan

13. Which team scored 260/6 against Kenya in the 2007 iteration of the T20 World Cup?
a. Bangladesh   b. Scotland   c. West Indies   d. Sri Lanka

14. How many runs were the Netherlands bowled out for at the 2014 T20 World Cup by Sri Lanka?
a. 28   b. 34   c. 39   d. 43

15. Which Australian bowler took the most wickets at the 2010 T20 World Cup?
a. Ryan Harris   b. Dirk Nannes   c. Shaun Tait   d. Brett Lee

16. Who was named Player of the Final in the 2022 T20 World Cup?
a. Sam Curran   b. Alex Hales   c. Jos Buttler   d. Mark Wood

17. Who is the only Bangladeshi player to score the most runs at a T20 World Cup, which he did so in 2016?

18. Which is the only player in T20 World Cup history to win back-to-back Player of the Tournament awards in 2014 and 2016?

19. How many times have New Zealand reached at least the semi-finals of the T20 World Cup?
a. 1   b. 2   c. 3   d. 4

20. Which country, that has never competed in the T20 World Cup, is due to co-host the 2024 iteration of the tournament?

21. How many teams are due to compete in the 2024 T20 World Cup?
a. 20   b. 24   c. 32

22. Scotland has appeared at how many T20 World Cups?
a. 2   b. 3   c. 5   d. 7

23. Sikandar Raza had the most sixes at the 2022 T20 World Cup, but how many did he score?
a. 9   b. 11   c. 13   d. 15

24. Which Pakistani bowler took the most wickets in the first two T20 World Cups?
a. Umar Gul   b. Shahid Afridi   c. Shadab Khan

25. Which England star was Player of the Final in 2010, but was forced to retire at the age of 27 when he was struck in the eye by a bail playing for his county?

ICC CRICKET WORLD CUP

1. In which year was the first ICC Cricket World Cup hosted?
a. 1973   b. 1975   c. 1977   d. 1979

2. Which nation hosted the first ICC Cricket World Cup?
a. Australia   b. South Africa   c. West Indies   d. England

3. Which competing nation did not play Test cricket at the time of the first ICC Cricket World Cup?
a. Zimbabwe   b. Bangladesh   c. Sri Lanka   d. Afghanistan

4. Which team lost in the final of the first ICC Cricket World Cup?
a. New Zealand   b. India   c. Pakistan   d. Australia

5. In the opening game of the first ICC Cricket World Cup, how many balls did Sunil Gavaskar face for his score of 36?
a. 16   b. 88   c. 137   d. 174

6. A team was entered into the first ICC Cricket World Cup comprised of players from four African nations: Kenya, Tanzania, Uganda and Zambia. What name did they compete under?

7. Which of the following non-Test-playing nations qualified for the ICC Cricket World Cup in 1979?
a. Scotland   b. United States   c. France   d. Canada

8. Who won the 1979 ICC Cricket World Cup?
a. West Indies   b. India   c. Pakistan   d. Australia

9. What were the first three ICC Cricket World Cups called due to the sponsor?
a. Kookaburra Championships   b. Gray-Nicholls Trophy
c. Prudential Cup   d. Black Cat Cup

10. How many overs did each side get in the first three ICC Cricket World Cups?
a. 40   b. 50   c. 60   d. 70

11. Which year did the ICC Cricket World Cup become a 50-over competition?
a. 1983   b. 1987   c. 1992   d. 1996

12. Which two countries hosted the 1987 ICC Cricket World Cup?

13. The 1992 ICC Cricket World Cup saw the swap from a red ball to which colour ball?

14. Why was South Africa banned from entering the ICC Cricket World Cup until the 1992 competition?

15. Who won the 1992 ICC Cricket World Cup?
a. Sri Lanka   b. West Indies   c. India   d. Pakistan

16. In which Asian city did Sri Lanka defeat Australia in the 1996 ICC Cricket World Cup final?

17. In which year did Australia claim their 3rd ICC Cricket World Cup in a row?
a. 1999   b. 2003   c. 2007   d. 2011

18. Which of the following teams did Australia NOT beat in the final of one of those 3 tournaments?
a. South Africa   b. India   c. Pakistan   d. Sri Lanka

19. Which associate country reached the ICC Cricket World Cup semi-finals in 2003?

20. Why was Pakistan stripped of hosting rights for the 2011 ICC Cricket World Cup?

21. Which African nation made its ICC Cricket World Cup debut in 2003?
a. Mozambique   b. Zimbabwe   c. Namibia   d. Ghana

22. Which Indian batter was voted Man of the Tournament after contributing 673 runs for his side in the 2003 ICC Cricket World Cup?

23. Which Australian bowler has taken the most wickets in the history of the competition?

24. How many times has Ricky Ponting captained Australia to ICC Cricket World Cup victory?
a. Once   b. Twice   c. Three times   d. Four times

25. Which Australian fast bowler took 27 wickets in one tournament in a year his side failed to even reach the final?
a. Mitchell Starc   b. Pat Cummins   c. Josh Hazelwood   d. Brett Lee

26. In which year was the Man of the Tournament award introduced to the ICC Cricket World Cup?
a. 1979   b. 1983   c. 1987   d. 1992

27. How many runs did Canada score against Sri Lanka in their fixture at the 2003 ICC Cricket World Cup?
a. 30   b. 36   c. 44   d. 51

28. Which Indian wicketkeeper/batter won Player of the Final as he captained his side to ICC Cricket World Cup glory in 2011?

29. How many times did England finish as runners-up before they won the ICC Cricket World Cup in 2019?
a. 1   b. 2   c. 3   d. 4

30. Which country is the only one to have competed in all ICC Cricket World Cups, up to and including 2019, but has not won it?
a. South Africa   b. Sri Lanka   c. Bangladesh   d. New Zealand

31. Which year was there an odd number of teams at the ICC Cricket World Cup?
a. 1987   b. 1992   c. 1996   d. 1999

32. Which year did Afghanistan first appear at the ICC Cricket World Cup?
a. 2007   b. 2011   c. 2015   d. 2019

33. Which two West Indies cricketers achieved the highest-ever partnership of 372 at the 2015 ICC Cricket World Cup?

34. How many ICC Cricket World Cup dismissals has Kumar Sangakkara been involved in as wicketkeeper?
a. 40   b. 54   c. 66   d. 75

35. Who was the first Man of the Tournament at the ICC Cricket World Cup?
a. Martin Crowe   b. Javed Miandad   c. Wasim Akram   d. Ian Botham

36. Viv Richards was the Man of the Match in the ICC Cricket World Cup final in 1979. How many runs de he score in the final?
a. 117   b. 138   c. 155   d. 180

37. Aravinda de Silva was Man of the Match in the ICC Cricket World Cup final in 1996 due to his all-round display of 107* runs, but what were his bowling figures?
a. 2/20   b. 2/45   c. 3/33   d. 3/42

38. How was the winner of the 2019 ICC Cricket World Cup decided?

39. Who captained England to victory at the ICC Cricket World Cup in 2019?

40. Which Australian all-rounder was Man of the Match in the ICC Cricket World Cup final in 2015?
a. James Faulkner   b. Michael Clarke
c. David Warner   d. Mitchell Marsh

41. How many runs did both sides score in the 2019 ICC Cricket World Cup final?
a. 197   b. 222   c. 241   d. 263

42. How many runs did both sides score in the 2019 ICC Cricket World Cup final Super Over?
a. 14   b. 15   c. 16   d. 18

43. Which side lost a wicket in their Super Over in the 2019 ICC Cricket World Cup final?

44. How many runs did Australia beat England by in the final of the 1987 ICC Cricket World Cup?
a. 3   b. 7   c. 12   d. 19

45. Who hosted the ICC Cricket World Cup in 2003, but were eliminated in the first round?

46. Sachin Tendulkar has scored how many runs at ICC Cricket World Cups?
a. 1,823   b. 1,992   c. 2,056   d. 2,278

47. In which year were coloured kits worn instead of the traditional cricket whites at the ICC Cricket World Cup?
a. 1992   b. 1996   c. 1999   d. 2003

48. How many times has Lords hosted the ICC Cricket World Cup final?
a. 3   b. 4   c. 5   d. 6

49. Which joint hosts contested the ICC Cricket World Cup final in 2011?

50. The ICC Cricket World Cup is due to expand again in 2027 to how many competing teams?
a. 12   b. 14   c. 16   d. 18

ICC CHAMPIONS TROPHY

1. How many overs are bowled in Champions Trophy matches?

2. Which country hosted the first Champions Trophy?
a. Pakistan   b. Bangladesh   c. South Africa   d. Sri Lanka

3. When was the first Champions Trophy tournament hosted?
a. 1996   b. 1998   c. 2000   d. 2002

4. Which two countries hosted back-to-back ICC Champions Trophies in 2013 & 2017?

5. Which nation won the inaugural ICC Champions Trophy?
a. India   b. Pakistan   c. Australia   d. South Africa

6. Which country won back-to-back ICC Champions Trophies in 2006 & 2009?
a. Australia   b. West Indies   c. India   d. New Zealand

7. India were the first team to score over how many runs in 1998 against Australia?
a. 200   b. 250   c. 300   d. 400

8. Which two countries were named co-champions of the 2002 ICC Champions Trophy after back-to-back wash outs?
a. Sri Lanka   b. Australia   c. England   d. West Indies   e. India

9. Which batter scored England's first 100 at an ICC Champions Trophy?
a. Andrew Flintoff   b. Marcus Trescothick
c. Michael Vaughan   d. Andrew Strauss

10. Who won the ICC Champions Trophy in 2017?
a. West Indies   b. Australia   c. New Zealand   d. Pakistan

11. Name the player who amassed 474 runs across the 2006 tournament, which was the most in the history of the tournament.

12. Who did Pakistan beat in the final of the 2017 ICC Champions Trophy by 180 runs?
a. Australia   b. New Zealand   c. West Indies   d. India

13. Who is the highest wicket-taker in ICC Champions Trophy history?
a. Kyle Mills   b. Muttiah Muralitharan
c. Lasith Malinga   d. Glenn McGrath

14. What figures did Farveez Maharoof achieve in an ICC Champions Trophy game against the West Indies in 2006?
a. 5/17   b. 5/24   c. 6/11   d. 6/14

15. Which South African all-rounder took the most wickets, won Player of the Tournament, and Player of the Final in the 1998 ICC Champions Trophy?

16. Which Indian batter scored the most runs in both the 2013 and 2017 ICC Champions Trophy tournaments?

17. Which Australian all-rounder won Player of the Final in successive tournaments in 2006 and 2009?
a. Michael Clarke   b. Shane Watson
c. Ricky Ponting   d. Mike Hussey

18. Which city hosted the first ever ICC Champions Trophy game?
a. Colombo   b. New Delhi   c. Dhaka   d. Karachi

19. What was the original name of the ICC Champions Trophy?

20. Which West Indies batter scored the most runs in the 1998 ICC Champions Trophy?
a. Brian Lara   b. Carl Hooper   c. Desmond Haynes   d. Philo Wallace

21. How many wickets did West Indies bowler Jerome Taylor take in the 2006 ICC Champions Trophy, which saw him take the most wickets in the tournament?
a. 13   b. 14   c. 15   d. 16

22. How many times have the USA competed in the ICC Champions Trophy?
a. 0   b. 1   c. 2   d. 3

23. Which nation hosted the 2006 ICC Champions Trophy?
a. South Africa   b. India   c. Pakistan   d. Kenya

24. Which year was decided by the Duckworth-Lewis Method?
a. 2004   b. 2006   c. 2009   d. 2013

25. How many times have England finished as runners-up in the ICC Champions Trophy?
a. 0   b. 1   c. 2   d. 3

1. What does BBL stand for?

2. Which nation hosts the IPL T20 competition?

3. In which year did the Caribbean Premier League first start?
a. 2010   b. 2012   c. 2013   d. 2015

4. Which of the following teams does not compete in the CPL?
a. Barbados Dynamites   b. Jamaica Tallawahs   c. Saint Lucia Kings

5. The Guyana Amazon Warriors have arguably been the best team in the CPL not to win the tournament. How many times have they finished second?
a. 3   b. 4   c. 5   d. 6

6. What is the name of the domestic T20 tournament in England?

7. Which nation was the second after England to host its own domestic T20 tournament?
a. New Zealand   b. India   c. Australia   d. West Indies

8. Which English bowler became the most expensive player of all time at the IPL 2023 auction?

9. In which city would you find the IPL headquarters?

10. Which team made its IPL debut in 2022 and amazingly won the title in the same year?
a. Lucknow Super Giants   b. Sunrisers Hyderbad   c. Gujarat Titans

11. Which city do the Rajasthan Royals play their home games at?
a. Jaipur   b. Ahmedabad   c. New Delhi   d. Guwahati

12. Which of the following teams that played in the inaugural season of the IPL is now defunct?
a. Deccan Chargers   b. Mumbai Indians
c. Chennai Super Kings   d. Royal Challengers Bangalore

13. Which former England & Sri Lanka coach is now the head coach of Punjab Kings?
a. Andy Flower   b. Trevor Bayliss   c. Mark Boucher

14. Which team is Ricky Ponting the head coach of in the IPL as of April 2023?

15. As of 2022, which team has won the most IPL titles of the 15 seasons played so far?
a. Chennai Super Kings   b. Mumbai Indians   c. Kolkata Knight Riders

16. A maximum of four overseas players are allowed in the playing XI in the IPL, but how many overseas players are allowed in the 25-player squads?
a. 5   b. 6   c. 7   d. 8

17. Each team is given a 'strategic timeout' in the IPL, but how long are these timeouts?
a. 2 minutes 30 seconds   b. 4 minutes   c. 6 minutes 30 seconds

18. Which Indian conglomerate provided the funding for the ICL - a rival league to the IPL?
a. TATA Consultancy Services   b. Zee Entertainment Enterprises
c. Hindustan Unilever   d. ICICI Bank

19. How many seasons did Kochi Tuskers Kerala compete in the IPL?
a. 1   b. 2   c. 4   d. 6

20. What was the original name of the Delhi Capitals?

21. What is the Orange Cap award given out for in the IPL?

22. Which Englishman got the MVP award for the 2022 IPL season?

23. Who were the title sponsors of the IPL between 2008-2012?
a. Mastercard   b. Ambuja Cements   c. Dream 11   d. DLF

24. Who is the 2022 and 2023 IPL sponsor?

25. How many of the following IPL teams are defunct? Kochi Tuskers Kerala, Gujarat Lions, Rising Pune Supergiant and Lucknow Super Giants.
a. 1   b. 2   c. 3   d. 4

26. Which Australian was the Player of the Series in the first iteration of the IPL?
a. Shane Watson   b. Michael Clarke   c. Steve Smith   d. Mike Hussey

27. Who were the first team to win back-to-back IPL titles?

28. Which team has lost 3 IPL finals between 2008 and 2022?

29. Which Jamaican has won the Player of the Series title twice?
a. Chris Gayle   b. Andre Russell   c. Sunil Narine   d. Dwayne Bravo

30. How many of their 14 normal season games did Kings XI Punjab win in 2014?
a. 11   b. 12   c. 13   d. 14

31. How many times has an Australian player been named Player of the Series in the IPL up to the end of the 2022 season?
a. 3   b. 4   c. 5   d. 6

32. How many teams competed in the 2013 IPL?
a. 8   b. 9   c. 10   d. 11

33. Which former Indian Test captain was the highest run scorer in the 2016 IPL with 973 runs?

34. The Australian T20 tournament, BBL, started in which year?
a. 2011   b. 2012   c. 2013   d. 2014

35. Who has the most runs in BBL history, with 3421 runs as of April 2023?
a. Jonathan Wells   b. D'Arcy Short   c. Glenn Maxwell   d. Chris Lynn

36. Which team won the inaugural season of the BBL, beating Perth Scorchers in the final by 7 wickets?
a. Brisbane Heat   b. Sydney Sixers
c. Adelaide Strikers   d. Hobart Hurricanes

37. What month of the year does the BBL start?
a. December   b. January   c. June   d. October

38. Who is the sponsor of the BBL until 2025?
a. McDonalds   b. Subway   c. KFC   d. Burger King

39. Which BBL team got the first three wooden spoon awards?
a. Adelaide Strikers   b. Melbourne Renegades   c. Sydney Thunder

40. How many BBL titles have Perth Scorchers won by the end of the 2023 season?
a. 3   b. 4   c. 5   d. 6

41. Who was the first player picked by the Melbourne Renegades in the 2022 draft?
a. Rashid Khan   b. Liam Livingstone
c. Sam Billings   d. Shadab Khan

42. Which Australian batter is the captain of the Brisbane Heat in the BBL?

43. As of April 2023, which player has taken the most wickets in the BBL?

44. Who were the first winners of the English T20 competition?
a. Somerset Sabres   b. Hampshire Royals
c. Leicestershire Foxes   d. Surrey Lions

45. Which English ground has hosted the T20 Blast final since 2013?
a. Edgbaston   b. Lords   c. The Oval

46. In which county are the Birmingham Bears based?
a. Leicestershire   b. Warwickshire   c. Oxfordshire   d. Staffordshire

47. Two teams have won the T20 Blast three times. Which two teams are they?
a. Leicestershire Foxes   b. Notts Outlaws
c. Hampshire Hawks   d. Kent Spitfires

48. Who was the Player of the Match when the Notts Outlaws were victorious in the final of the 2017 T20 Blast against the Birmingham Bears?
a. Alex Hales   b. Samit Patel   c. Harry Gurney

49. Hampshire Hawks won by how many runs in the 2022 T20 Blast final?
a. 1 run   b. 2 runs   c. 4 runs   d. 8 runs

50. What is the T20 Blast name for the Lancashire based team?

NEW FORMATS

1. The Hundred is a new format of domestic cricket that is hosted in which country?

2. After how many balls do they switch what end they are bowling from in The Hundred?
a. 8   b. 10   c. 12   d. 20

3. In which year did The Hundred begin?
a. 2018   b. 2019   c. 2020   d. 2021

4. What is the maximum amount of balls a bowler can bowl in The Hundred?
a. 10   b. 15   c. 20   d. 30

5. What type of illegal delivery is worth 2 runs and a free hit in The Hundred?

6. How many overseas players are allowed in each The Hundred squad?
a. 2   b. 4   c. 5   d. 6

7. Which women's The Hundred team won back-to-back titles in 2021 and 2022?
a. London Spirit   b. Manchester Originals
c. Birmingham Phoenix   d. Oval Invincibles

8. The first-ever domestic T10 tournament was held in which year?
a. 2012   b. 2014   c. 2015   d. 2017

9. Which country was the first to host a T10 tournament?

10. How many teams competed in the 2022 T10 European Cricket League?
a. 15   b. 20   c. 25   d. 30

11. What is the name of the T10 side in Abu Dhabi that England international Moeen Ali is captain of?
a. Team Abu Dhabi   b. New York Strikers   c. Morrisville Samp Army

12. How many overseas players are allowed in a team of 11 in the Abu Dhabi T10 tournament?
a. 4   b. 6   c. 8   d. 10

13. Which former Somerset county cricketer was the leading wicket-taker in the 2021 Abu Dhabi T10 tournament with 12 wickets?

14. The 6IXTY is a T10 tournament held in which country?
a. Barbados   b. Saint Kitts & Nevis   c. Trinidad and Tobago

15. How many wickets does the batting side have to lose to be all out in 6IXTY in comparison to standard T10 cricket?
a. 6   b. 7   c. 8   d. 9

16. In which month of the year is the Qatar T10 league played?
a. June   b. September   c. December   d. March

17. Which Australian batter scored the most runs in the 2019 Abu Dhabi T10 tournament?
a. Chris Lynn   b. Eoin Morgan   c. Shane Watson   d. Andre Russell

18. What is the name of the team that finished as runners-up in the Abu Dhabi T10 tournament in 2018?
a. Northern Warriors   b. Kerala Kings   c. Pakhtoons

19. Which team won the men's The Hundred in 2022?
a. Trent Rockets   b. Manchester Originals   c. Southern Brave

20. How many runs did Dawid Malan score in the 2022 The Hundred tournament?
a. 290   b. 312   c. 349   d. 377

21. How many balls did Liam Livingstone face on his way to scoring the most runs, being 348, in the 2021 edition of The Hundred?
a. 146   b. 195   c. 230

22. Two players were tied for the most sixes with 20 in the 2022 The Hundred. Which of the following two players were they?
a. Adam Lyth   b. David Weise   c. Faf du Plesis   d. Dawid Malan

23. Who was the leading wicket-taker in the women's The Hundred in 2021?
a. Tash Farrant   b. Sammy-Jo Johnson   c. Kirstie Gordon

24. Which player scored the most fifties in the women's The Hundred in 2021?
a. Evelyn Jones   b. Sophia Dunkley   c. Jemimah Rodrigues

25. Which team finished runner-up in both 2021 and 2022 in the women's The Hundred?
a. Trent Rockets   b. Welsh Fire   c. London Spirit   d. Southern Brave

FIRST CLASS CRICKET

1. Which English first-class county club was founded first in 1836?
a. Hampshire   b. Sussex   c. Kent   d. Surrey

2. Which of the English first-class counties is actually based in Wales?

3. How many days must a game be to be considered first-class cricket?
a. 2   b. 3   c. 4   d. 5

4. What is the first-class competition called in England?

5. How many first-class counties compete in the English competition?
a. 14   b. 16   c. 18   d. 20

6. How many times have Warwickshire won the County Championship?
a. 3   b. 6   c. 8   d. 11

7. What is the first-class competition called in Australia?
a. Sheffield Shield   b. Cairns Championship   c. Australia Trophy

8. How many points does a team get for a win in the Australian first-class competition?
a. 3   b. 4   c. 5   d. 6

9. How many teams play in the Australian first-class competition?
a. 4   b. 6   c. 10   d. 14

10. Who were the first winners of the Australian first-class competition?
a. Western Australia   b. Victoria   c. Queensland   d. Tasmania

11. Which Australian international cricketer won Player of the Year in 2020/21 in the Australian first-class competition?
a. Peter Siddle   b. Mitchell Marsh   c. Nathan Lyon

12. The CSA 4-Day Domestic Series started in which year?
a. 1868   b. 1889   c. 1912   b. 1929

13. How many teams competed in the 2022–23 CSA 4-Day Series?
a. 11   b. 13   c. 15   d. 17

14. Which player has scored the most runs in CSA 4-Day Domestic Series history with 12,409?
a. Graeme Pollock   b. Graeme Smith   c. Henry Fotheringham

15. Who was the highest run scorer in the 2015/16 CSA 4-Day Domestic Series (then known as the Sunfoil Series)?
a. Henry Davids   b. Dwaine Pretorius
c. Imraan Khan   d. Heino Kuhn

16. Which player holds the record for the most runs in a single innings in CSA 4-Day Domestic Series?
a. Rilee Rossouw   b. Allan Lamb   c. Stephen Cook

17. Who has the most wickets in the history of the CSA 4-Day Domestic Series, with 572?
a. Dale Steyn   b. Vintcent van der Bijl   c. Morne Morkel

18. How many points does a team get for a win in the CSA 4-Day Domestic Series?
a. 6   b. 10   c. 12   d. 16

19. The Ranji Trophy is a first-class competition based in which nation?
a. Pakistan   b. Bangladesh   c. Sri Lanka   d. India

20. How many teams compete for the Ranji Trophy?
a. 24   b. 32   c. 38   d. 44

21. What is the format of the Ranji Trophy?
a. Knockout   b. Double round-robin then knockout
c. League   d. Round-robin then knockout

22. How many times have Delhi won the Ranji Trophy?
a. 7   b. 12   c. 17   d. 22

23. Which team scored the largest total in Ranji Trophy history with 944/6d in 1993/94?
a. Mumbai   b. Bangalore   c. Chennai   d. Hyderbad

24. Hyderbad had the lowest team score in the Ranji Trophy in 2010 with how many runs?
a. 21   b. 27   c. 35   d. 41

25. VVS Laxman has the most runs in a single season of Ranji Trophy cricket. In which season did he achieve this?
a. 1994/95   b. 1997/98   c. 1999/00   d. 2002/03

26. Which Indian bowler has the record for the best bowling figures in a Ranji Trophy match of 16/99?
a. Javagal Srinath   b. Harbhajan Singh   c. Anil Kumble   d. Kapil Dev

27. Which player holds the record for most runs, most centuries and most games played in the Ranji Trophy?
a. Rahul Dravid   b. Sachin Tendulkar   c. Wasim Jaffer

28. Which team won the first ever Ranji Trophy in 1934/35?
a. Hyderabad   b. Bombay   c. Western India   d. Gujarat

29. Which team won their first ever Ranji Trophy in 2017?
a. Gujarat   b. Chennai   c. Haryana   d. Vidarbha

30. The Plunket Shield is a first-class competition held in which nation?

31. Who are the most successful team in terms of title wins in the Plunket Shield?
a. Wellington   b. Auckland   c. Otago   d. Canterbury

32. How many points are awarded for a win in the Plunket Shield?
a. 6   b. 8   c. 12   d. 16

33. Which player took the most wickets in the Plunket Shield from 2015/16 to 2017/18?
a. Neil Wagner   b. Ajaz Patel   c. Kyle Mills   d. Trent Boult

34. Which of the following are the last three counties yet to win the English County Championship?
a. Gloucestershire   b. Hampshire   c. Glamorgan
d. Northamptonshire   e. Somerset   f. Worcestershire

35. How many reasons are there for points deductions in the County Championship?
a. 4   b. 5   c. 7   d. 10

36. Which county holds the record for the highest team score in one innings of the County Championship of 887?
a. Surrey   b. Yorkshire   c. Kent   d. Essex

37. Which batter has the highest individual score in the County Championship of 501 not out?
a. W.G. Grace   b. George Hirst   c. Bill Ponsford   d. Brian Lara

38. Which insurance company began sponsoring the County Championship for the second time in 2021?

39. Which player has the record for most runs in the County Championship, with 46,268?
a. Phil Mead   b. Jack Hobbs   c. Herbert Sutcliffe   d. Frank Woolley

40. Which player has the record for the most wickets in the County Championship, with 3,151?
a. Johnny Briggs   b. Brian Statham
c. Tich Freeman   d. Johnny Briggs

ENGLAND CRICKET

1. In which nation was England's 2019 World Cup winning captain born?
a. South Africa   b. New Zealand   c. Ireland   d. Australia

2. Players born in which other nation play for England?
a. Wales   b. Scotland   c. Northern Ireland   d. Ireland

3. When did the ECB take over from MCC and become England's governing body?
a. 1994   b. 1995   c. 1996   d. 1997

4. Who captained the England team when they won the 2010 World Twenty20?
a. Andrew Strauss   b. Kevin Pietersen
c. Stuart Broad   d. Paul Collingwood

5. How many Test matches has England played up to the end of 2022?
a. 876   b. 1,058   c. 1,597   d. 1845

6. In which year was the selection committee put in place to pick the England team?
a. 1883   b. 1899   c. 1922   d. 1937

7. Who is England's highest wicket-taker in ODI's?
a. Darren Gough   b. James Anderson
c. Stuart Broad   d. Andrew Flintoff

8. What was the series score when England first played South Africa in 1905/06?
a. 3-1 England   b. 2-2 tied   c. 4-1 South Africa

9. Which British paper published an obituary of the England cricket team after losing their first Test series at home?
a. Private Eye   b. The Sporting Times   c. The Sun   d. The Daily mail

10. Which England batter scored 287 runs on his debut, helping England to regain the Ashes in 1904?
a. Pelham Warner   b. Reginald Erskine Foster   c. Jack Hobbs

11. Which monarch became the first King or Queen of England to watch Test cricket in 1912?

12. Where did England go on their final tour before the start of the First World War, where they won the series 4-0?
a. India   b. Pakistan   c. South Africa   d. New Zealand

13. How many times has the Ashes been drawn?
a. 4   b. 6   c. 8   d. 10

14. Of the 131 Test matches played against India, how many has England won?
a. 42   b. 50   c. 61   d. 70

15. England sent separate teams to both the West Indies and which other nation whilst on tour in 1929/30?
a. South Africa   b. India   c. New Zealand   d. Australia

16. When did England first play Ireland in a Test match?
a. 2019   b. 2020   c. 2021   d. 2022

17. England's highest successful run chase came in 2022, where the target set was 378. Against which team was this?

18. England's fewest runs in an innings in the 21st century so far came in 2009, where they scored a meagre 51 runs. Against which team was this?
a. India   b. Australia   c. Pakistan   d. West Indies

19. Who was England's first Test after the Second World War against?
a. South Africa   b. West Indies   c. Australia   d. India

20. How many times have England won a Test match by a margin of 10 wickets?
a. 20   b. 26   c. 34   d. 42

21. England has played over 100 Test matches against all of the following teams. Put them in order of their win percentage from highest to lowest: South Africa, New Zealand, West Indies.

22. How many Tests did England go unbeaten from 1968 to 1971?
a. 19   b. 22   c. 24   d. 27

23. Who was the England captain during this period?
a. Brian Close   b. Ray Illingworth   c. Mike Brearley   d. Peter May

24. Tony Greig was sacked from his position as England captain for his involvement in which cricket tournament?

25. Who took over as captain after Greig's sacking as England's captain?
a. Mike Brearley   b. Basil D'Oliveria   c. Geoffrey Boycott

26. Winning a Test by one wicket is extremely rare. How many times have England won by just one wicket?
a. 1   b. 4   c. 6   d. 9

27. Between September 1985 and July 1990, what was the only nation that England beat at home?
a. West Indies   b. Bangladesh   c. Sri Lanka   d. South Africa

28. Who were England's opponents when Botham was stripped of his England captaincy mid-series?

29. Which bowler took over the England captaincy in 1982?
a. David Gower   b. Graham Gooch   c. Bob Willis   d. Mike Brearley

30. Sri Lanka inflicted the third-worst defeat in England's Test history in the third Test in 2003. Sri Lanka won by an innings and how many runs?
a. 172 runs   b. 190 runs   c. 215 runs   d. 248 runs

31. Who replaced Graham Gooch as captain in 1993 after a miserable run of results?
a. Nasser Hussain   b. Michael Atherton   c. Alec Stewart

32. Which former captain was the coach during this period?
a. Tony Greig   b. Mike Brearley   c. Ray Illingworth

33. Which nation broke off from the England cricket team in 1992 to compete separately?

34. When he made his Test debut in 1991, what was Mark Ramprakash's number cap?
a. Cap 549   b. Cap 632   c. Cap 708

35. In which year did England first reach the top of the ICC rankings?
a. 2009   b. 2010   c. 2011   d. 2012

36. England have lost a Test match by a margin of 10 wickets on 25 different occasions. How many other Test-playing teams have lost by this margin more times than England?
a. 0   b. 1   c. 2   d. 3

37. What type of contract was brought in to reduce the England player's workloads in the year 2000?

38. In which year was Duncan Fletcher appointed as England's coach?
a. 1997   b. 1999   c. 2001   d. 2003

39. Michael Vaughan captained England in 51 Tests. How many of these did England win?
a. 20   b. 23   c. 26   d. 30

40. Who became the first Sikh to represent England in the summer of 2006?

41. Which future captain and opening batsman also made his England debut in 2006, after impressing for Essex?

42. Who succeed Duncan Fletcher as England coach after he resigned?
a. David Lloyd   b. Andy Flower   c. Peter Moores

43. Who was England's captain between Vaughan and Strauss?

44. Alastair Cook scored how many runs in the 2010-2011 Ashes to be named Man of the Series?
a. 650   b. 766   c. 823   d. 892

45. Who has the individual highest score for the England Test side?
a. Graham Gooch   b. Alastair Cook
c. Wally Hammond   d. Len Hutton

46. How many runs did the person from question 45 score?
a. 329   b. 364   c. 398   d. 433

47. Alastair Cook led England to their first series victory in India for how many years in 2012?
a. 28   b. 34   c. 40   d. 47

48. Joe Root ranks in second place for most career Test runs for England. How many runs did he score in total?
a. 8,420   b. 9,745   c. 10,948   d. 12,005

49. Which bowler holds the unfortunate record of the most ducks in England Test history?
a. James Anderson   b. John Snow
c. Stuart Broad   d. Steve Harmison

50. What is England's highest team total in Test matches?
a. 645-5dec   b. 778-4dec   c. 831-9dec   d. 903-7dec

SCANDALS & CONTROVERSY

1. IPL 'Slap Gate' saw a confrontation between which two players?

2. Why were the Chennai Super Kings and Rajasthan Royals suspended for two seasons in 2015?

3. Which England captain was the subject of 'text gate' that saw Kevin Pietersen send texts about the captain to the South African team in 2012?
a. Michael Vaughan   b. Alastair Cook
c. Paul Collingwood   d. Andrew Strauss

4. Herschelle Gibbs described the leaders within the South African team, led by Graeme Smith, as what in his book titled To The Point?
a. Schoolchildren   b. A Clique   c. Arrogant   d. Corrupt

5. Which umpire first no-balled Muttiah Muralitharan for his action at the 1995 Boxing Day Test between Australia and Sri Lanka?
a. David Evans   b. Darrell Hair   c. Frank Farrands

6. Which former Australia ODI captain ordered his brother Trevor to bowl an underarm delivery to stop New Zealand from tying the game?

7. How long was Shane Warne banned after testing positive for banned diuretic during the 2003 World Cup?
a. 1 month   b. 3 months   c. 6 months   d. 1 year

8. Which Indian off-spinner was subject to a 3-match ban after Australia captain, Ricky Ponting, reported the bowler's behaviour to umpires during a Test at the SCG in 2008?
a. Harbhajan Singh   b. Ravindra Jadeja
c. Kuldeep Yadav   d. Axar Patel

9. Marlon Samuels was banned for 2 years for what indiscretion?
a. Doping   b. Ball-tampering   c. Physical altercation   d. Corruption

10. Which Gujarat cricketer turned bookie got a 5-year ban for an IPL spot-fixing scandal in 2013?
a. Arun Jaitley   b. Niranjan Shah   c. Amit Singh

11. Three Pakistani Test players were jailed for taking bribes in a game against England in 2010. Which player received the longest sentence of 30 months?
a. Salman Butt   b. Mohamad Amir   c. Mohammad Asif

12. Which two Australian Test players were investigated for potential bribery charges in 1998 after rumours about them accepting bribes from Indian bookmakers about team selection in 1994/95?
a. Glenn McGrath   b. Shane Warne   c. Mark Waugh
d. Ricky Ponting   e. Adam Gilchrist

13. Which former Pakistan coach sadly died at the 2007 World Cup?
a. Javed Miandad   b. Waqar Younis
c. Mushtaq Ahmed   d. Bob Woolmer

14. Which visiting team were subject to a terrorist attack in Pakistan in 2009 en route to the Gaddafi Stadium in Lahore?
a. Bangladesh   b. England   c. Sri Lanka   d. West Indies

15. Which former South African ODI captain was banned for life after pleading guilty to match-fixing in 2002?
a. Kepler Wessels   b. Hansie Cronje
c. Shaun Pollock   d. Graeme Smith

16. Why did Andy Flower and Henry Olonga wear black armbands at the 2003 World Cup?

17. Which England captain was fined for ball tampering in a Test against South Africa at Lords in 1994?
a. Michael Atherton   b. Alec Stewart
c. Michael Vaughan   d. Nasser Hussain

18. Who was the South African Prime Minister turned President who refused the England cricket team entry to the country if they brought Basil D'Oliveira in 1968?
a. Nicolaas Johannes Diederichs
b. Jacobus Johannes Fouché
c. Balthazar Johannes Vorster

19. What was the name of the match referee who banned 6 Indian players in 2001 after what he described as 'bad behaviour'?
a. Mike Denness   b. Mel Johnson   c. Steve Woodward

20. The Indian cricket board protested decisions made by which highly respected umpire in the 2008 Test against Australia, which saw him removed for the following Test in Perth?
a. Simon Taufel   b. Steve Bucknor   c. Aleem Dar   d. Marais Erasmus

21. Umpire Shakoor Rana accused which England captain of altering the field, as a bowler ran in to bowl in a Test in Pakistan in 1987?
a. Michael Atherton   b. Mike Gatting   c. Ian Botham

22. Australia's Dennis Lillee walked out to bat at the WACA against England in 1979 with a bat made of what material?
a. Carbon fiber   b. Bamboo   c. Aluminium   d. Plastic

23. In what year was England bowler John Snow grabbed by a member of the Australian crowd after hitting Terry Jenner with a bouncer?
a. 1955   b. 1963   c. 1971   d. 1980

24. Which Australian wicketkeeper was fined 75% of his match fee after being caught attempting to alter the condition of the ball with sandpaper in South Africa in 2018?

25. Which Australian captain resigned from his position in November 2021 due to an investigation by the Australia cricket board into texts he sent 4 years prior, to a co-worker?

PLAYER RECORDS

1. Sunil Gavaskar scored how many runs in Test match cricket?
a. 7,845   b. 8,502   c. 9,302   d. 10,122

2. How many wickets did Anil Kumble take how in Test match cricket?
a. 619   b. 703   c. 845   d. 898

3. Graham Gooch scored how many runs in Test match cricket?
a. 8,145   b. 8,900   c. 9,602   d. 10,023

4. Dale Steyn took how many wickets in Test match cricket?
a. 373   b. 407   c. 439   d. 482

5. AB de Villiers scored how many runs in Test match cricket?
a. 8,765   b. 9,245   c. 9,825   d. 10,201

6. Michael Holding took how many wickets in Test match cricket?
a. 182   b. 249   c. 294   d. 362

7. Michael Vaughan scored how many runs in Test match cricket?
a. 5,229   b. 5,719   c. 6,338   d. 6,845

8. Richard Benaud took how many wickets in Test match cricket?
a. 211   b. 248   c. 290   d. 352

9. Thilan Samaraweera scored how many runs in Test match cricket?
a. 4,102   b. 4,699   c. 5,017   d. 5,462

10. Zaheer Khan took how many wickets in Test match cricket?
a. 190   b. 228   c. 274   d. 311

11. Marcus Trescothick scored how many runs in Test match cricket?
a. 5,825   b. 6,900   c. 7,797   d. 8,211

12. Morne Morkel took how many wickets in Test match cricket?
a. 245   b. 309   c. 380   d. 461

13. Richard Richardson scored how many runs in Test match cricket?
a. 4,599   b. 5,103   c. 5,949   d. 6,812

14. Robert Willis took how many wickets in Test match cricket?
a. 191   b. 227   c. 268   d. 325

15. Carl Hooper scored how many runs in Test match cricket?
a. 4,611   b. 5,762   c. 6,670   d. 7,093

16. Richard Hadlee took how many wickets in Test match cricket?
a. 431   b. 490   c. 570   d. 612

17. Justin Langer scored how many runs in Test match cricket?
a. 5,333   b. 5,914   c. 6,559   d. 7,696

18. Makhaya Ntini took how many wickets in Test match cricket?
a. 390   b. 435   c. 480   d. 525

19. Sourav Ganguly scored how many runs in Test match cricket?
a. 6,712   b. 7,212   c. 7,755   d. 8,097

20. Allan Donald took how many wickets in Test match cricket?
a. 284   b. 330   c. 391   d. 452

21. Alan Knott had how many dismissals in Test match cricket?
a. 191   b. 219   c. 241   d. 269

22. Andrew Flower had how many dismissals in Test match cricket?
a. 151   b. 177   c. 193   d. 243

23. Godfrey Evans had how many dismissals in Test match cricket?
a. 170   b. 219   c. 291   d. 339

24. BJ Watling had how many dismissals in Test match cricket?
a. 210   b. 257   c. 299   d. 346

25. Ian Healy had how many dismissals in Test match cricket?
a. 395   b. 462   c. 506   d. 539

GENERAL FACTS

1. What colour ball is used in a day/night Test match?
a. Orange   b. Yellow   c. Green   d. Pink

2. What are the dimensions of a cricket wicket?
a. 20 yards by 10 feet   b. 22 yards by 10 feet   c. 22 yards by 12 feet

3. Which former Pakistani player served as his country's Prime Minister?

4. What is used as a tie-breaker when a limited-overs match of cricket is drawn?

5. According to the Guinness World Records, how many days did the longest cricket match in history last, which later became known as the 'Timeless Test'?
a. 8 days   b. 10 days   c. 12 days   d. 14 days

6. In which year was Ben Stokes born?
a. 1987   b. 1989   c. 1991   d. 1993

7. Which player was the first in history to score a century?
a. Charles Bannerman   b. Arthur Shrewsbury   c. J.J. Ferris

8. Which two nations competed in the first-ever international cricket match?
a. England & Australia   b. England & South Africa
c. USA & Canada   d. England & India

9. Which wood are cricket bats traditionally made from?

10. Until 1889, how many balls were bowled per over?
a. 3   b. 4   c. 5   d. 8

11. What colour ball was used in the early days of women's cricket?
a. Black   b. Green   c. Yellow   d. Blue

12. Until what year did women wear skirts while playing cricket?
a. 1964   b. 1975   c. 1986   d. 1997

13. Edgar Willsher was the first bowler to bowl what type of ball?

14. If a bowler takes a hat trick, what have they done?

15. In which year was the first documented game of cricket in India?
a. 1721   b. 1743   c. 1757   d. 1778

16. Which of the following is reported to be the oldest cricket club in the world?
a. Marylebone Cricket Club
b. Mitcham Cricket Club
c. Hellingly Cricket Club

17. What does ICC stand for?

18. Which Asian country became a full member of the ICC in 1926?

19. Which two countries have complete 'veto' rights for the ICC?

20. In which year did Brian Lara make his Test debut?
a. 1990   b. 1992   c. 1994   d. 1996

21. Where was the first ever One-Day international game played under floodlights in 1979?
a. Sydney   b. London   c. Colombo   d. Kingston

22. Name the stadium in Sheffield which has hosted one England Test match.

23. In which year did India first play in Delhi, against the West Indies?
a. 1942   b. 1948   c. 1956   d. 1962

24. Cricket has been involved in the Olympics just once. In which year did this happen?
a. 1900   b. 1948   c. 1992   d. 2012

25. In which country were the 1998 commonwealth games held, which included cricket for the first time?
a. Australia   b. Scotland   c. India   d. Malaysia

26. Which nation won the only ever cricket Olympic gold medal?
a. Australia   b. France   c. Great Britain   d. South Africa

27. Which form of dismissal was introduced to the game in 1774?
a. Hit the ball twice   b. Leg before wicket (LBW)
c. Stumped   d. Timed out

28. In which year did the Aboriginal Australian side first tour England?
a. 1848   b. 1868   c. 1888   d. 1908

29. What width were cricket bats limited to in 1771?
a. 4 and 1/4 inches   b. 4 and 3/4 inches   c. 5 and 1/4 inches

30. In which year was Jack Hobbs born?
a. 1875   b. 1882   c. 1891   d. 1899

31. Which umpire has officiated the most Test matches in history?
a. Aleem Dar   b. Rudi Koertzen   c. David Shepherd

32. The first cricket balls had a core, wound with string, and a leather cover stitched on. What was the core made from?
a. Foam   b. Ball bearings   c. Oak   d. Cork

33. Which nation was the first to play 1000 Test matches?
a. Australia   b. England   c. India   d. West Indies

34. Who was the first player to score a six on the first ball of a Test match?
a. Ben Stokes   b. Brendon McCullum   c. Chris Gayle

35. How many Tests did Adam Gilchrist play in a row after his debut in 1999?
a. 22   b. 49   c. 77   d. 96

36. Which Indian bowler dropped Alastair Cook, Brendon McCullum and Michael Clarke in their highest-scoring innings?
a. Ashish Nehra   b. R. P. Singh   c. Ishant Sharma   d. Irfan Pathan

37. Which of the following former New Zealand Test bowlers took more wickets than he scored runs?
a. Trent Boult   b. Chris Cairns   c. Chris Martin

38. Which Indian player won 4 consecutive Player of the Match awards in ODIs?
a. Sourav Ganguly   b. Sachin Tendulkar   c. Rahul Dravid

39. Which two nations has Dirk Nannes represented at international level?

40. In which year did MS Dhoni make his cricket debut?
a. 2001   b. 2003   c. 2005   d. 2007

41. How many 6's did Sir Donald Bradman score in his Test career?
a. 6   b. 22   c. 31   d. 45

42. Who is the only player in Test history to captain his nation for over 100 Tests?
a. Graeme Smith   b. Allan Border   c. Clive Lloyd   d. Virat Kohli

43. What is the approximate number of people that play/watch cricket worldwide, which puts it as the second most popular sport in the world?
a. 1.1 Billion   b. 1.6 Billion   c. 2.2 Billion   d. 2.5 Billion

44. How many stumps were used until 1775 when it was changed to 3?
a. 1   b. 2   c. 4   d. 5

45. What age did Sachin Tendulkar make his Test debut for India?
a. 15   b. 16   c. 17   d. 18

46. A run out of the non-striker by the bowler before bowling the ball, if the non-striker leaves their crease too early, is known as what?

47. How old was England's oldest-ever player, Will Rhodes, when he made his final-ever Test appearance?
a. 44   b. 47   c. 49   d. 52

48. Which of the following two scores are thought to be unlucky?
a. 27   b. 56   c. 87   d. 111

49. What is on-field banter between players called in cricket?
a. Jumbling   b. Borking   c. Sledging   d. Flaxing

50. Who became Australian Test captain in 2021?

HISTORY OF CRICKET

1. Which two teams played out the first draw in Test match cricket in 1960?
a. India & West Indies   b. England & Australia
c. South Africa & England   d. Australia & West Indies

2. True or false: versions of cricket have been documented as far back as the 16th century.

3. Which batter was the first in history to score centuries in both innings of a Test match?
a. Jack Blackham   b. Alick Bannerman   c. Warren Bardsley

4. Who was the first batter to score a triple hundred in a Test match?
a. Andy Sandham   b. Brian Lara
c. Donald Bradman   d. David Warner

5. Who did New Zealand beat in their first Test match win in 1956?
a. England   b. West Indies   c. India   d. South Africa

6. Which Indian batter scored the most runs in the decade of the 1970s?
a. Gundappa Viswanath   b. Kapil Dev
c. Dilip Vengsarkar   d. Sunil Gavaskar

7. Which Australian batter scored the most runs in the decade of the 1980s?
a. Allan Border   b. Steve Waugh   c. David Boon   d. Greg Chappell

8. Which English batter scored the most runs in the decade of the 1990s?
a. Michael Atherton   b. Graham Gooch
c. Alec Stewart   d. Graham Thorpe

9. When was cricket first introduced to Australia?
a. 1754   b. 1788   c. 1812   d. 1839

10. Which Australian took the first hat-trick in Test cricket in 1879?
a. Thomas Garrett   b. Frederick Spofforth   c. Francis Allan

11. Graham Thorpe was on the opposition on both occasions as which West Indies batter broke the record for the most runs in a single innings in 1994 and then broke his own record again in 2004?

12. Which batter scored the first-ever runs in Test match cricket?
a. Fred Grace   b. Jack Blackham   c. Charles Bannerman

13. Which nation was the 10th to become a Test-playing side?
a. Zimbabwe   b. Sri Lanka   c. Ireland   d. Bangladesh

14. Which cricketer is nicknamed the 'Little Master'?

15. Otto Nothling replaced which legendary Australian batter for one Test in December 1928?
a. Bill Ponsford   b. Don Bradman   c. Jack Fingleton

16. In which year did Pakistan make its Test debut?
a. 1948   b. 1952   c. 1958   d. 1961

17. In which year in England did all first-class cricketers become professional by default?
a. 1951   b. 1956   c. 1959   d. 1963

18. Waqar Younis was the only player not to be dismissed by which Indian bowler when he took all 10 wickets in an innings in 1999?

19. Which of the following Pakistani batters scored 1788 Test runs in 2006?
a. Saeed Anwar   b. Inzamam-ul-Haq   c. Mohammad Yousuf

20. How many Test match centuries did Sir Donald Bradman score?
a. 20   b. 29   c. 37

21. Who was the first batsman to score one hundred sixes in Test cricket?
a. Chris Gayle   b. Brendon McCullum   c. Adam Gilchrist

22. Len Hutton is the only batter in Test match history to be given out for what reason?

23. Which former Indian wicketkeeper has the record for the highest score in an ODIs by a wicketkeeper?
a. Syed Kirmani   b. Wriddhiman Saha   c. MS Dhoni   d. Kiran More

24. Which international team used four different wicketkeepers in a single innings of a Test match in 1986?
a. Pakistan   b. South Africa   c. Australia   d. England

25. When did the first match take place at Edgbaston Cricket Ground, where they played MCC, which was watched by over 3000 spectators?
a. 1886   b. 1896   c. 1906   d. 1916

26. Until which decade was the ball delivered along the ground in cricket?
a. 1690s   b. 1710s   c. 1740s   d. 1760s

27. Which cricket club moved to Lords cricket ground in 1787?

28. In 1836 a match took place in England where all counties combined together to make two teams to play against each other. What were the two sides called?

29. In which year was South Africa welcomed back into the international cricket scene, following their suspension due to apartheid?
a. 1987   b. 1989   c. 1991   d. 1993

30. When was the first series of the women's Ashes played?
a. 1919   b. 1928   c. 1934   d. 1946

31. In which nation were Kevin Pietersen and Jonathan Trott born? (Both went on to represent England at Test match level)

32. In which year did the MCC change the rules, meaning that the bowler's hand at the time of delivery must not be above their shoulder?
a. 1835   b. 1854   c. 1872   d. 1891

33. In which year were the first laws of cricket written?
a. 1701   b. 1732   c. 1744   d. 1756

34. What Anglo-Saxon word is believed to be the origin of the name cricket, which was the word for a shepherd's staff?
a. Coket   b. Cricc   c. Cralk   d. Crook

35. Shoaib Akhtar holds the record for the fastest delivery of all time with a speed of 161.3 kph (100.2 mph). In which year did he achieve this?
a. 1999   b. 2003   c. 2006   d. 2008

ANSWERS

TERMINOLOGY

1. All-rounder
2. Number of times the batter is out
3. Runs scored when the ball does not make contact with any part of the batter
4. b - An opening batsman is not dismissed when the team innings closes
5. Wicket-keeper
6. Declaration
7. a - 0
8. a - Doosra
9. Duckworth-Lewis-Stern method (DLS)
10. Economy Rate
11. A maiden over is when the bowler does not concede a single run in that over
12. Net Run Rate
13. c - One short
14. Sight screens
15. a - Slip
16. Test
17. Timed out
18. Decision Review System
19. Umpires
20. That it is easy for batting
21. b - 3
22. Bouncer
23. The captain
24. d - Cow corner
25. When it swings both ways (In & Out) in the same delivery

STADIUMS

1. Lords
2. d - 132,000
3. c - 7
4. a - Brisbane
5. b - 1956
6. d - Eden Park
7. a - Barbados
8. Old Trafford
9. b - South Africa
10. b - Sri Lanka
11. Sophia Gardens
12. Wankhede Stadium
13. a - Sabina Park
14. Stadium Australia
15. Earthquake
16. d - Birmingham
17. Nepal
18. c - Southampton
19. Optus Stadium
20. Sydney Thunder

GUESS THE PLAYER

1. b - Kevin Pietersen
2. c - Adam Gilchrist
3. b - Mahela Jayawardene
4. a - Courtney Walsh
5. c - Steve Harmison
6. a - David Gower
7. Sachin Tendulkar
8. d - Ricky Ponting
9. Jimmy Anderson
10. b - Daniel Vettori
11. a - Jason Gillespie
12. Shane Warne
13. Garry Sobers
14. Dale Steyn
15. c - Fred Trueman
16. c - Glenn McGrath
17. Wasim Akram
18. Ian Botham
19. d - Waqar Younis
20. Dennis Lillee
21. b - Aaron Finch
22. c - Younis khan
23. Moeen Ali
24. d - Clive Lloyd
25. Curtly Ambrose

GUESS THE MATCH

1. a - Pakistan, 2022
2. d - Sri Lanka, 2010
3. c - South Africa, 1994
4. a - England, 2012
5. d - Australia, 2015
6. d - Pakistan, 2004
7. b - Pakistan, 2014
8. d - India, 2014
9. b - Sri Lanka, 1982
10. c - Australia, 2001
11. d - Pakistan, 2016
12. a - England, 2003
13. d - South Africa, 2008
14. b - West Indies, 2015
15. d - England, 1994
16. c - Bangladesh, 2012
17. a - West Indies, 1988
18. d - Zimbabwe, 1998
19. b - New Zealand, 2000
20. d - Pakistan, 2016
21. c - England, 2000
22. b - South Africa, 2016
23. a - England, 1976
24. c - Australia, 1928
25. b - Zimbabwe, 2003

THE ASHES

1. b - 5
2. c - 2013
3. Matthew Prior
4. d - Don Bradman
5. Richie Benaud
6. Lords Cricket Ground (Museum)
7. a - Merv Hughes
8. d - Terry Alderman
9. d - 905
10. Terracotta
11. b - 1882
12. a - The Oval, London
13. England
14. d - Ivo Bligh
15. c - 8
16. c - 3
17. b - Allan Border
18. c - 2013-14
19. b - 2
20. a - Mike Gatting
21. Jim Laker
22. b - Gary Pratt
23. a - Ashton Agar
24. d - Eric Hollies
25. b - They played on separate pitches
26. a - Sir Len Hutton
27. d - 7
28. b - 89.78
29. a - 2-1 England
30. The ashes of a set of bails, or the ashes of a burnt lady's veil
31. c - Shane Warne
32. c - Sydney Barnes

33. b - Allan Border
34. a - 21
35. Nasser Hussein
36. c - An innings and 322
37. c - 37
38. b - 135*
39. MCG
40. b - Billy Midwinter
41. c - Sabotaging the pitch
42. b - Sammy Woods
43. a - Tom Veivers
44. Jason Gillespie
45. d - 423
46. d - 22
47. d - Nathan Lyon
48. b - George McShane
49. c - Grade 3
50. b - Clarrie Grimmett

WORLD TEST CHAMPIONSHIP

1. c - 2019
2. d - 2021
3. a - New Zealand
4. b - Kyle Jamieson
5. c - Joe Root
6. Rose Bowl, Southampton, England
7. b - Ravichandran Ashwin
8. d - 2013
9. a - 4th August 2021
10. d - Axar Patel

T20 WORLD CUP

1. b - India
2. b - South Africa
3. c - 24
4. c - 2007
5. a - England
6. b - 3
7. Kensington Oval, Bridgetown, Barbados
8. d - Brendon McCullum
9. c - Chris Gayle
10. Jos Buttler & Alex Hales
11. a - Wanindu Hasaranga
12. c - Tillakaratne Dilshan
13. d - Sri Lanka
14. c - 39
15. b - Dirk Nannes
16. a - Sam Curran
17. Tamim Iqbal
18. Virat Kohli
19. d - 4
20. United States of America
21. a - 20
22. c - 5
23. b - 11
24. a - Umar Gul
25. Craig Kieswetter

ICC CRICKET WORLD CUP

1. b - 1975
2. d - England
3. c - Sri Lanka
4. d - Australia
5. d - 174
6. East Africa
7. d - Canada
8. a - West Indies
9. c - Prudential Cup
10. c - 60
11. b - 1987
12. India & Pakistan
13. White
14. Apartheid
15. d - Pakistan
16. Gaddafi Stadium, Lahore, Pakistan
17. c - 2007
18. a - South Africa
19. Kenya
20. There was a terrorist attack on the Sri Lankan team, so they were stripped based on security concerns
21. c - Namibia
22. Sachin Tendulkar
23. Glenn McGrath
24. b - Twice
25. a - Mitchell Starc
26. d - 1992
27. b - 36
28. MS Dhoni
29. c - 3
30. d - New Zealand

31. b - 1992
32. c - 2015
33. Chris Gayle & Marlon Samuels
34. b - 54
35. a - Martin Crowe
36. b - 138
37. d - 3/42
38. Boundaries scored
39. Eoin Morgan
40. a - James Faulkner
41. c - 241
42. b - 15
43. New Zealand
44. b - 7
45. South Africa
46. d - 2,278
47. a - 1992
48. c - 5
49. India & Sri Lanka
50. b - 14

ICC CHAMPIONS TROPHY

1. 50 Overs
2. b - Bangladesh
3. b - 1998
4. England & Wales
5. d - South Africa
6. a - Australia
7. c - 300
8. a & e - Sri Lanka & India
9. b - Marcus Trescothick
10. d - Pakistan
11. Chris Gayle
12. d - India
13. a - Kyle Mills
14. d - 6/14
15. Jacques Kallis
16. Shikhar Dhawan
17. b - Shane Watson
18. c - Dhaka
19. ICC Knockout Trophy
20. d - Philo Wallace
21. a - 13
22. b - 1
23. b - India
24. b - 2006
25. c - 2

Domestic T20

1. Big Bash League
2. India
3. c - 2013
4. a - Barbados Dynamites
5. c - 5
6. T20 Blast
7. a - New Zealand
8. Sam Curran
9. Mumbai, India
10. c - Gujarat Titans
11. a - Jaipur
12. a - Deccan Chargers
13. b - Trevor Bayliss
14. Delhi Capitals
15. b - Mumbai Indians
16. d - 8 players
17. a - 2 minutes 30 seconds
18. b - Zee Entertainment Enterprises
19. a - 1 season
20. Delhi Daredevils
21. IPL top run scorer
22. Jos Buttler
23. d - Delhi Land & Furniture (DLF)
24. TATA
25. c - The three defunct teams are Kochi Tuskers Kerala, Gujarat Lions and Rising Pune Supergiant
26. a - Shane Watson
27. Chennai Super Kings (2010 & 2011)
28. Royal Challengers Bangalore
29. b - Andre Russell
30. a - 11
31. b - 4
32. b - 9

33. Virat Kohli
34. a - 2011
35. d - Chris Lynn
36. b - Sydney Sixers
37. a - December
38. c - KFC
39. c - Sydney Thunder
40. c - 5
41. b - Liam Livingstone
42. Usman Khawaja
43. Sean Abbott
44. d - Surrey Lions
45. a - Edgbaston
46. b - Warwickshire
47. a & c - Leicestershire Foxes and Hampshire Hawks
48. b - Samit Patel
49. a - 1 run
50. Lancashire Lightning

NEW FORMATS

1. England
2. b - 10 balls
3. d - 2021
4. c - 20 balls
5. A no ball
6. b - 4
7. d - Oval Invincibles
8. d - 2017
9. United Arab Emirates
10. d - 30 teams
11. c - Morrisville Samp Army
12. d - 10 out of 11
13. Jamie Overton
14. b - Saint Kitts & Nevis
15. a - 6
16. c - December
17. a - Chris Lynn
18. c - Pakhtoons
19. a - Trent Rockets
20. d - 377
21. b - 195
22. a & d - Adam Lyth & Dawid Malan
23. a - Tash Farrant
24. c - Jemimah Rodrigues
25. d - Southern Brave

First Class Cricket

1. b - Sussex
2. Glamorgan
3. b - 3 days
4. The County Championship
5. c - 18 counties
6. c - 8
7. a - Sheffield Shield
8. d - 6
9. b - 6
10. b - Victoria
11. c - Nathan Lyon
12. b - 1889
13. c - 15
14. a - Graeme Pollock
15. d - Heino Kuhn
16. c - Stephen Cook
17. b - Vintcent van der Bijl
18. d - 16 points
19. d - India
20. c - 38
21. d - Round-robin then knockout
22. a - 7
23. d - Hyderbad
24. a - 21
25. c - 1999/00
26. c - Anil Kumble
27. c - Wasim Jaffer
28. b - Bombay
29. a - Gujarat
30. New Zealand
31. b - Auckland
32. c - 12 points

33. b - Ajaz Patel
34. a, d & e - Gloucestershire, Northamptonshire and Somerset
35. c - 7
36. b - Yorkshire
37. d - Brian Lara
38. LV
39. a - Phil Mead
40. c - Tich Freeman

ENGLAND CRICKET

1. c - Ireland
2. a - Wales
3. d - 1997
4. d - Paul Collingwood
5. b - 1,058
6. b - 1899
7. b - James Anderson
8. c - 4-1 South Africa
9. b - The Sporting Times
10. b - Reginald Erskine Foster
11. King George V
12. c - South Africa
13. b - 6
14. b - 50
15. c - New Zealand
16. a - 2019
17. India
18. d - West Indies
19. d - India
20. a - 20
21. First with a 46.42% win percentage is New Zealand, second with a win percentage of 42.31% is South Africa, third with a win percentage of 31.28% is the West Indies
22. d - 27
23. b - Ray Illingworth
24. World Series Cricket
25. a - Mike Brearley
26. b - 4
27. c - Sri Lanka
28. Australia
29. c - Bob Willis
30. c - 215 runs

31. b - Michael Atherton
32. c - Ray Illingworth
33. Scotland
34. a - Cap 549
35. c - 2011
36. a - 0
37. Central contracts
38. b - 1999
39. c - 26
40. Monty Panesar
41. Alastair Cook
42. c - Peter Moores
43. Kevin Pietersen
44. b - 766
45. d - Len Hutton
46. b - 364
47. a - 28
48. c - 10,948
49. c - Stuart Broad
50. d - 903-7dec

SCANDALS & CONTROVERSY

1. Harbhajan Singh & Shanthakumaran Sreesanth
2. Spot-fixing (betting scandal)
3. d - Andrew Strauss
4. b - A Clique
5. b - Darrell Hair
6. Greg Chappell
7. d - 1 Year
8. a - Harbhajan Singh
9. d - Corruption
10. c - Amit Singh
11. a - Salman Butt
12. b & c - Shane Warne & Mark Waugh
13. d - Bob Woolmer
14. c - Sri Lanka
15. b - Hansie Cronje
16. To protest Robert Mugabe
17. a - Michael Atherton
18. c - Balthazar Johannes Vorster
19. a - Mike Denness
20. b - Steve Bucknor
21. b - Mike Gatting
22. c - Aluminium
23. c - 1971
24. Cameron Bancroft
25. Tim Paine

PLAYER RECORDS

1. d - 10,122
2. a - 619
3. b - 8,900
4. c - 439
5. a - 8,765
6. b - 249
7. b - 5,719
8. b - 248
9. d - 5,462
10. d - 311
11. a - 5,825
12. b - 309
13. c - 5,949
14. d - 325
15. b - 5,762
16. a - 431
17. d - 7,696
18. a - 390
19. b - 7,212
20. b - 330
21. d - 269
22. a - 151
23. b - 219
24. b - 257
25. a - 395

General Facts

1. d - Pink
2. b - 22 yards by 10 feet
3. Imran Khan
4. Super Over
5. b - 10 days
6. c - 1991
7. a - Charles Bannerman
8. c - USA & Canada
9. Willow
10. b - 4
11. d - Blue
12. d - 1997
13. Overarm
14. Taken 3 wickets in 3 consecutive balls
15. a - 1721
16. b - Mitcham Cricket Club
17. International Cricket Council
18. India
19. England & Australia
20. a - 1990
21. a - Sydney
22. Bramall Lane
23. b - 1948
24. a - 1900
25. d - Malaysia
26. c - Great Britain
27. b - Leg Before Wicket or LBW
28. b - 1868
29. a - 4 and 1/4 inches
30. b - 1882
31. a - Aleem Dar
32. d - Cork

33. b - England
34. c - Chris Gayle
35. d - 96
36. c - Ishant Sharma
37. c - Chris Martin
38. a - Sourav Ganguly
39. Australia & The Netherlands
40. c - 2005
41. a - 6
42. a - Graeme Smith
43. d - 2.5 Billion
44. b - 2
45. b - 16
46. Mankad
47. d - 52 years old
48. c & d - 87 is 13 short of 100, and 111 looks like stumps with no bails on
49. c - Sledging
50. Pat Cummins

HISTORY OF CRICKET

1. d - Australia & West Indies
2. True
3. c - Warren Bardsley
4. a - Andy Sandham
5. b - West Indies
6. d - Sunil Gavaskar
7. a - Allan Border
8. c - Alec Stewart
9. b - 1788
10. b - Frederick Spofforth
11. Brian Lara
12. c - Charles Bannerman
13. d - Bangladesh
14. Sachin Tendulkar
15. b - Don Bradman
16. b - 1952
17. d - 1963
18. Anil Kumble
19. c - Mohammad Yousuf
20. b - 29
21. c - Adam Gilchrist
22. Obstructing the Field
23. c - MS Dhoni
24. d - England
25. a - 1886
26. d - 1760s
27. Marylebone Cricket Club (MCC)
28. North Counties & South Counties
29. c - 1991
30. c - 1934
31. South Africa
32. a - 1835

33. c - 1744
34. b - Cricc
35. b - 2003

Printed in Great Britain
by Amazon

37503136R00051